Printing

Sue Nicholson

QEB Publishing

Copyright © QEB Publishing, Inc. 2005

Published in the United States by
QEB Publishing, Inc.
23062 La Cadena Drive
Laguna Hills, CA 92653

www.qeb-publishing.com

Library of Congress Control Number: 2005921164

ISBN 1-59566-080-1

Written by Sue Nicholson
Designed by Susi Martin
Photography Michael Wicks
Editor Paul Manning

Publisher Steve Evans
Creative Director Louise Morley
Editorial Manager Jean Coppendale

The author and publisher would like to
thank Emily and Millie, and Sarah Morley,
for making the models.

Printed and bound in China

Note to teachers and parents/carers

The projects in this book are aimed at children in
grades 1–3 and are presented in order of difficulty—
from easy to more challenging. Each can be used
as a stand-alone activity or as part of another area
of study.

While the ideas here are offered as inspiration,
children should always be encouraged to work
from their imagination and first-hand observation.

All projects in this book require adult supervision.

Sourcing ideas

★ Encourage children to source ideas from their own
  experiences, as well as from books, magazines,
  the Internet, galleries, or museums.
★ Prompt them to talk about different types of art
  they have seen at home or on vacation.

★ Use the "Click for Art!" boxes as a starting point
  for finding useful material on the Internet.*
★ Suggest that each child keeps a sketchbook
  of their ideas and their favorite prints.

Evaluating work

★ Encourage children to share and compare their
  work with others. What do they like best/least
  about it? If they did the project again, what
  would they do differently?
★ Help children to judge the originality of their
  work and to appreciate the different qualities
  in others' work. This will help them to value ways
  of working that are different from their own.
★ Encourage children by displaying their work.

* Website information is correct at the time of going to
  press. However, the publishers cannot accept liability
  for information or links found on third-party websites.

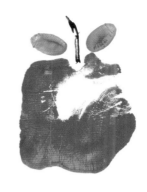

Contents

Words in bold, **like this**, are explained in the Glossary on page 24.

Getting started

This book will show you how to make fantastic prints from cardboard, sponges, leaves—even food. Here are some of the things you will need:

Basic equipment
- Paper and cardboard
- Poster/**acrylic** paints
- Pencils and paintbrushes
- Safety scissors
- White glue
- Ruler

You will also need the extra items listed separately for each project.

Paper
You can make prints on white or colored paper, cardstock, posterboard, or cardboard.

Printing blocks
You can make **printing blocks** from craft foam, sponges, or cardboard.

Paints for printing

The best paints to use are poster paints or acrylic paints. Use fabric paints for printing on cloth.

Don't forget to spread some newspaper to work on, and to wear an apron to keep your clothes clean.

Take care!

Some projects involve cutting, ironing, and photocopying. Always ask an adult for help where you see this sign:

Craft supplies

Keep a big box full of things you can use to make prints. Look out for items with interesting **textures** or shapes. For example:

★ the end of heavyweight corrugated cardboard
★ an old sponge or cork
★ a piece of yarn
★ bubble wrap
★ a Lego® brick
★ a feather

Brushes and paint dishes

You will need different-size paintbrushes and old dishes for mixing your paints.

A **printing roller** is also useful for spreading paint evenly on a flat surface.

Body prints

You can make fantastic prints with your hands or fingertips! Just follow these easy steps.

Top tip
Keep a bowl of soapy water and a towel handy. Clean your fingers before you dip them in a new color.

Butterfly frieze

1 Paint green grass and blue sky on a large sheet of paper and leave it to dry.

You will need:
- A large sheet of white paper
- Some white poster-board
- Felt-tip pen or pipe cleaners

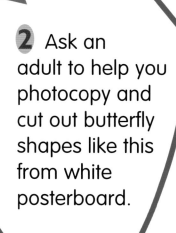

2 Ask an adult to help you photocopy and cut out butterfly shapes like this from white posterboard.

Apple prints

1 Paint your palm with red paint and press it onto paper.

2 Make a brown stalk by printing with the side of a short piece of cardboard.

3 Press your thumb into green paint to print leaves.

3 Dip your fingertips in paint and press them onto the cut-out butterfly shapes.

4 Glue the shapes onto the background. Draw feelers with a felt-tip pen, or glue on pipe cleaners.

Use your fingertips to print these fun animals, then add details with a felt-tip pen.

Click for Art!

To see ancient handprints on cave walls in Australia, go to
www.dvc.vic.gov.au/aav/heritage/mini-posters/14RockArt.pdf

7

Leaf prints

This project shows you how to make a printed leaf border for a picture or poem.

1 To make the border, draw a straight line 2½in (6cm) in from each side of your sheet of construction paper or posterboard. Ask an adult to cut out the middle section for you.

2 Paint the underside of a leaf and press it onto the frame in one corner.

3 Use the same leaf to make prints in the other corners. Coat the leaf with fresh paint each time.

You will need:
- A selection of clean, dry leaves
- Construction paper or posterboard 10 x 12in (25 x 30cm)

4 Build up a **pattern** of leaf shapes in different colors all around the frame. Try beech, sycamore, and oak leaves.

8

Click for Art!

To see leaf designs by William Morris, visit **www.morrissociety.org** Click on the designs and follow the links.

Top tips

- Make a test print on scrap paper first.
- Leave one color to dry before you add the next.

flowers printed from a real flower head

When your border is dry, glue your picture or poem behind it, or use it as a photo frame.

Nature prints

Try making prints with:
- ★ twigs and bark
- ★ flowers
- ★ the underside of a mushroom

stems printed from twigs

Junk prints

Pieces of junk, such as nails, screws, cardboard, or thread spools make great prints. But always ask before you use them!

Here are some things to try:

★ **Corrugated** cardboard
★ An empty toilet-paper roll
★ A scrunched-up paper bag
★ Nails, screws, or washers
★ An old sponge or cork
★ A Lego® brick or puzzle piece

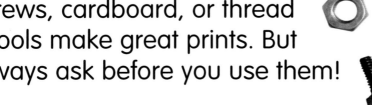

screw heads

How to make a printing pad

Printing pads use less paint and make a clearer, cleaner print.

Top tip
Don't forget that you will need to make a separate pad for each color.

I Ask an adult to help you cut a piece of foam to fit in the bottom of a plastic bowl. The easiest way is to place the bowl on top of the foam and draw around it first.

2 Pour enough paint into the bowl to cover the bottom. Leave it until the foam soaks up the paint.

10

stamping robot

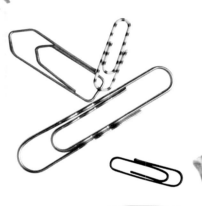

plastic bottlecap

Build up your picture from pieces of junk. Print the junk on scrap paper first to see how it looks.

corrugated cardboard

cork

bubble wrap

Lego® brick

3 Press your piece of junk onto the foam, and then press it onto a sheet of paper to make your print.

Food prints

Print with fruit or vegetables onto fabric to make fun placemats. Ask an adult to help you with cutting and slicing your food.

You will need:
- Food for printing
- Fabric paints
- Pinking shears
- Plain muslin cloth

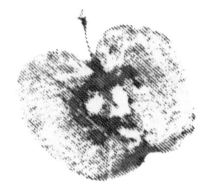

Food shapes and patterns

Look for food with interesting patterns or shapes:

★ Dried pasta shapes, such as wheels, long tubes, or butterflies

★ A piece of broccoli or cauliflower

★ Half an apple or orange

★ A large cabbage leaf

★ A slice of carrot or celery

★ Half a bell pepper

1 Set out the food you are going to print with and some dishes of fabric paint. Sketch your rough design on paper first.

2 Ask an adult to help you cut the fabric for the placemats into rectangles 12 x 10 in (30 x 25 cm). Use pinking shears so the edges don't fray.

Fabric paints

- Be sure to let each color dry before you add an overlapping one.
- Most fabric paints need pressing with a hot iron to stop the colors from washing out. Ask an adult to do this for you.

Click for Art! To learn all about traditional block printing on fabric in India, go to **www.sashaworld.com/block/block.htm**

Top tip

Wipe the cut surface of fruit or vegetables dry before you paint it. This helps the paint stick better and you will make a clearer print.

3 Dip the food into the paint, or paint the surface of the food with a brush. Press down firmly on the cloth to make the print.

Block prints

You can make a printing block by gluing a foam shape to cardboard or a small block of wood. Printing blocks can be used over and over again.

You will need:
- Craft foam
- Cardboard, wood, or an empty matchbox for the block

1 Draw a simple shape on a piece of craft foam and ask an adult to help you cut it out.

Top tip
If you want to overlap colors, let one color dry before you print the next.

2 Glue the foam shape to a small block of wood, an empty matchbox, or layers of cardboard glued together.

3 With a brush, paint the shape with poster or acrylic paint.

4 Press the shape onto paper to make a **repeat pattern**.

A simple repeat pattern using one block

A repeat pattern using two blocks

An overlapped pattern using two blocks

Click for Art!

To see Japanese woodblock prints, go to **www.cjn.or.jp/ukiyo-e/arts-index.html** To see a woodcut from Aesop's *Fables*, go to **www.wolmanprints.com/pages/single/all/b/404344.html**

String prints

Make simple printing blocks by gluing string to small pieces of cardboard or wood. The results are amazing!

You will need:
- Paper or posterboard
- A piece of wood, cardboard, or a piece of styrofoam for the block
- String

1 Paint a blue watery background onto paper or posterboard.

Top tip
Sprinkle a little salt onto the blue paint while wet. This will give the background an interesting grainy texture.

2 When the paint is dry, print tall green reeds with the edge of a long piece of cardboard.

3 Glue string to the printing block in a fish shape. Make a large fish block and a smaller one.

4 Glue on string for the fish's scales. Make an eye from string glued in a spiral or a circle of foam.

5 Paint the printing block and press onto the background. Paint the block each time you print.

Simple blocks

You can glue all kinds of things to wood or cardboard to make printing blocks:
★ Grains of rice
★ Nails, screws, or washers
★ Buttons
★ A feather
★ Paperclips
★ An old key

Print fish swimming in the same direction like real fish.

Print reeds behind and on top of the fish, so the fish appear to be swimming through them.

Stencil prints

Cards decorated with **stencils** are easy to make—and fun to send to your friends!

You will need:

- Plain and colored cardstock
- Thin card for the stencil
- A thick paintbrush

1 Choose a shape that is **symmetrical**—the same on both sides.

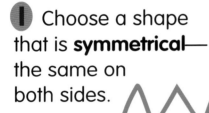

2 Fold a small square of cardstock in half. Draw half the design at the fold.

3 Carefully cut out your stencil and open it out.

4 Fold a sheet of colored cardstock in half lengthwise.

5 Hold your stencil firmly over the front of the card and dab paint through the stencil with a thick bristly brush.

Top tip

Use a little paint at a time so it does not leak under the stencil.

Wrapping paper and gift tags

Print stencils in a regular pattern onto plain paper to make a sheet of wrapping paper.

Print a stencil onto a square of cardstock and hole-punch it to make a matching gift tag.

Click for Art!

To see stencils by Yoshitoshi Mori, go to **www.castlefinearts.com/catalog.aspx?catID=97**.

One-off prints

A **monotype** is a one-off print made by pressing a sheet of paper over a painted picture or design.

Scraper prints

1 Using a brush or a printing roller, cover a flat surface thickly with paint.

2 Make a pattern in the paint with a pencil or cotton swab, or drag a cardboard comb across the surface.

Stencil monotype

This one-off print of a boat at sea was made by rolling paint over cut-out shapes. A cardboard comb was then dragged through the paint to make the waves.

Top tip

Instead of a desk or mirror, work on a sheet of polythene plastic. Tape the sides down with masking tape so it doesn't move.

Click for Art!

To see **monotype** prints, go to **www.artlex.com** Click on "-Mz page," scroll down to "monotype," then click on the print titles.

3 While the paint is still wet, press a clean sheet of paper onto your design. Smooth the paper down with your hands or use a clean printing roller.

4 Gently lift up the paper. Be very careful not to smudge it. Leave the picture on a flat surface to dry.

21

Marbling

In marbling, a beautiful print is made from swirling oil paint dripped into water. Oil and water don't mix, so the oil paint stays on the surface and sticks to the paper.

You will need:

- A large shallow bowl or tray (such as an old plastic bowl or a baking pan)
- Oil paints and **mineral spirits**
- Pencil, stick, or straw
- Heavyweight white paper

1 Fill your bowl or pan almost to the top with water.

2 With an adult mix the paint with mineral spirits until the paint is runny. ⚠

22

Marbled collage

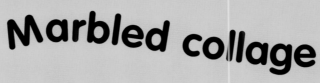

Top tip

When marbling, use just two colors to start with. If you use too many, they will mix together and become muddy.

Cut shapes of marbled paper and stick them onto a background of different-colored paper so the pictures stand out.

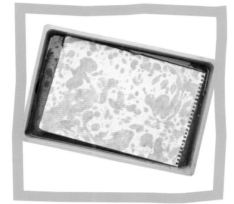

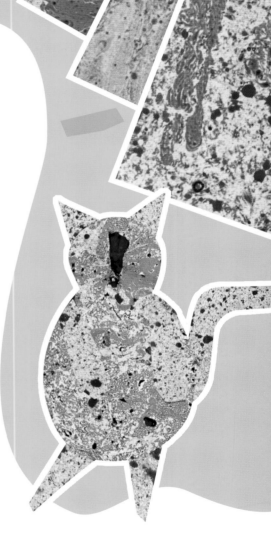

3 Drop tiny blobs of paint onto the water's surface and gently swirl the colors around with a pencil or a stick.

4 Lay your paper on the water's surface. Make sure there are no air bubbles trapped underneath.

Top tip

Instead of stirring the paint with a pencil, try blowing it around the bowl through a straw.

5 Leave for a few seconds, then gently remove the paper. Place the marbled paper on a flat surface to dry.

Click for Art!

To see beautiful examples of marbled paper, go to **http://members.aol.com/marbling/marbling**. Click on "28 Examples of marbling."

Glossary

acrylic   easy-to-mix paint that can be cleaned with soap and water

construction paper   thick, textured paper often used in scrapbooks

corrugated   type of cardboard with a pattern of ridges and grooves

mineral spirits   liquid used to make oil-based paint more runny

monotype   one-off print made by pressing a sheet of paper over a painted picture or design

pattern   repetition of shape, line or colour in a design

printing block   object to which paint is applied to make a print

printing roller   tool used to spread paint or ink evenly over the surface to be decorated such as paper

repeat pattern   pattern that has the same shapes, lines or colours used over and over again

stencil   shape cut out of thin card which you can paint or print through

symmetrical   shape that is the same on both sides

texture   surface or 'feel' of something

Index